Published in 2013 by The Rosen Publishing Group, Inc.
29 East 21st Street, New York, NY 10010

Photo Credits: **KEY** tl=top left; tc=top center; tr=top right; cl=center left; c=center; cr=center right; bl=bottom left; bc=bottom center; br=bottom right; bg=background

CBT = Corbis; GI = Getty Images; iS = istockphoto.com;
TF = Topfoto; TPL = photolibrary.com; wiki = Wikipedia

8bl, cl, cr iS; **9**bl, cr, tr iS; **10**bl iS; **14**cl CBT; bl iS; **19**br iS; **20**br CBT; **20-21**bc wiki; **21**tl, tr iS; **24**cl, bg iS; **24-25**c GI; tc iS; **25**cr, tr CBT; cr, bg iS; br TPL; **26-27**bg iS; cl TF; **27**tc CBT; bc, bl, br, c, tc, tl, tr iS; bl, br, cr, cl TF; **28**bc, bg, c, cr iS; bc TPL; **28-29**c, c, tc, tc, bc, bc iS; **29**br, bg iS

All illustrations copyright Weldon Owen Pty Ltd

Weldon Owen Pty Ltd
Managing Director: Kay Scarlett
Creative Director: Sue Burk
Publisher: Helen Bateman
Senior Vice President, International Sales: Stuart Laurence
Vice President Sales North America: Ellen Towell
Administration Manager, International Sales: Kristine Ravn

Library of Congress Cataloging-in-Publication Data

Costain, Meredith.
  The end of Pompeii / by Meredith Costain.
      p. cm. — (Discovery education: ancient civilizations)
  Includes index.
  ISBN 978-1-4777-0048-8 (library binding) — ISBN 978-1-4777-0081-5 (pbk.) —
  ISBN 978-1-4777-0082-2 (6-pack)
  1. Pompeii (Extinct city)–History. 2. Pompeii (Extinct city)—Social life and customs. 3. Excavations (Archaeology)—Italy—Pompeii (Extinct city) 4. Italy—Antiquities, Roman. I. Title.
  DG70.P7C69 2013
  937'.7256807—dc23
                                    2012019584

Manufactured in the United States of America

CPSIA Compliance Information: Batch #W13PK2: For Further Information contact Rosen Publishing, New York, New York at 1-800-237-9932

THE END OF POMPEII

MEREDITH COSTAIN

PowerKiDS press
New York

Contents

Life in Ancient Rome

Rome was a large, noisy city, filled with beautiful temples and important public buildings. People dodged chariots as they hurried through the crowded streets, on their way to work or school. The streets and lanes were lined with shops and apartment buildings. The rich lived in gracious homes and kept slaves to do everything they wanted them to do.

Roman soldier
Ancient Rome had a trained army that marched into new countries and conquered them for the Roman Empire. The army had foot soldiers, who were called legionnaires, and cavalry units on horseback.

Helmet

Spear

Armor

Shiel

Rome

ITALY

Pompeii

From Rome to Pompeii
Rome was the center of the Roman Empire. Pompeii was a city located about 130 miles (210 km) southeast of Rome.

Who's who in Roman society

The emperor and his family were at the top of Roman society, while slaves were at the bottom. In between them were the upper and lower classes.

Emperor's wife

Although the wife of the emperor had no power, she was treated with great respect by the people of Rome. She wore beautiful clothes and lived in luxury.

Emperor

The emperor was the most powerful person in Rome. Everyone had to obey him. He wore a brightly colored and embroidered toga, which was called a toga picta.

Senator

Members of the upper class were known as patricians. The men could become members of the Senate and take part in the government of the empire.

Slave

Slaves were the property of their owners and had very few rights. Although some slaves were given their freedom eventually, most remained slaves for their entire life.

Plebeian

The members of the lower class of citizens were called plebeians or plebs. They included most people in Rome, from merchants to freed slaves.

Before the Eruption

Like other ancient Roman cities, Pompeii was laid out in a grid pattern, with houses and apartment blocks lining the streets. It was surrounded by a wall that had seven gates. The streets were paved with blocks of lava, with raised sidewalks for pedestrians. Sewers carried running water to private bathrooms in wealthy homes. Poorer citizens had to make do with public baths in the streets. In the center of Pompeii was the forum, an open square, surrounded by public buildings. There were law courts and offices, a gladiators' court, temples, and public bathhouses. The walls of the richest citizens' homes were covered with colorful paintings of local gods and goddesses.

The city of Pompeii

In 27 BC, the wealthy city of Pompeii came under the rule of Augustus, the first Roman emperor. It was a busy place of at least 12,000 people. Many were merchants or shopkeepers.

Insulae

People lived in crowded apartment buildings called insulae. They were usually three or four stories high.

Transporting goods

Horses and mules were used to transport goods on carts around the city. Oxen were yoked to carts or wagons. Slaves also carried packs or pulled wagons laden with goods.

Street vendors

Because very few homes had kitchens, most people bought their food already cooked from food stalls or street vendors. Some people cooked in the street using portable stoves.

Balconies
Many of the insulae had balconies, where people could sit outside in the fresh air or hang out their washing.

Shops
There were no supermarkets in Pompeii. People went to small shops that specialized in particular goods.

Water
Water fountains at every crossroad were fed by supplies of clean freshwater from local aqueducts.

The Eruption

Movement of Earth's tectonic plates below the Mediterranean Sea causes volcanoes to erupt along the sea's northern shores, and earthquakes to shake the area. There are two main groups of volcanoes in the Mediterranean: one in and around Italy, the other in the Greek Islands. At about 1:00 p.m. on August 24, AD 79, the volcano Mount Vesuvius, which was located 5 miles (8 km) from Pompeii, blew its top. It sent tons (t) of molten ash, mud, and sulfuric gas into the atmosphere. By the next day, pyroclastic flows from the volcano had swamped the city, burying it under more than 10 feet (3 m) of ash and pumice.

That's Amazing!
Before Mount Vesuvius blew in AD 79, local people did not know it was a volcano. It had not erupted for 300 years. Then Pompeii was buried deeply, and people forgot it had ever existed.

Sleeping dragon
Mount Vesuvius has erupted many times, although not since 1944. Mount Etna, on the Italian island of Sicily, erupts every few years. Vesuvius is a major threat to the city of Naples, which lies at the foot of the mountain.

Panic in Pompeii

Mount Vesuvius erupted with a mighty blast, shooting fire, smoke, and ash into the sky. The city was bombarded by volcanic stones and the air filled with ash. Shouting and screaming, the people of Pompeii gathered whatever belongings they could carry and ran out into the streets, desperate to escape.

Ashfall
Herculaneum was
completely buried
beneath ash and
other volcanic debris
that rained down
from the sky.

The only escape
The people living in
Herculaneum fled to
the boathouses of the
port town, hoping to
escape by sea.

Escape or Perish

The volcanic eruption lasted for more than 24 hours. Only those who fled in the first few hours had any chance of survival. The people in the nearby port town of Herculaneum rushed to the boathouses, clutching their jewelry and money, desperate to escape. But there were not enough boats for everyone. By midnight, a devastating avalanche of hot ash, pumice, rock fragments, and lethal volcanic gas had engulfed first Herculaneum and then later, Pompeii.

Putting to sea
Getting on a boat was a dangerous option, but it offered the only escape route for the desperate people of Herculaneum.

Reading the past
In the 1980s, archaeologists digging in the ruins of Herculaneum discovered about 250 human skeletons. They were huddled inside the vaulted arcades of boathouses, which had once lined the shore. These discoveries have helped scientists to recreate what happened that day in Herculaneum. Most people would have died quickly from the intense heat that shrouded the town.

Dangerous waters
The eruption caused violent winds and earthquakes, which created turbulent seas in the Bay of Naples.

Timetable of Destruction

Mount Vesuvius is one of the world's most dangerous volcanoes. Several violent eruptions occurred before the explosion that buried Pompeii, including an eruption in about 1800 BC that engulfed several villages. Since AD 79, the volcano has erupted repeatedly, most recently in 1944. All these eruptions have varied greatly in their size and severity, but all were a Plinian type of eruption. This has a column of gas and ash that shoots miles (km) into the air. It is named after Pliny the Younger, who witnessed the eruption in AD 79.

> The death toll for the region was estimated to have been between 3,000 and 10,000 people.

Recording history
Gaius Plinius Caecilius Secundus (AD 61–115), known as Pliny the Younger, was a Roman official, lawyer, and writer. His letters are an important source of Roman history.

" *... the cloud stretched down to the ground and covered the sea.* "
PLINY THE YOUNGER

Major eruptions throughout history
The eruption should have been no surprise. However, the local people were unaware of Vesuvius's history of violent eruptions and did not realize that a series of recent tremors meant it was about to blow again.

16,300 BC: Basal Pumice eruption
This was the first Plinian-type eruption of Mount Vesuvius. It was followed by a series of less powerful eruptions.

14,000 BC: Green Pumice eruption
This was the second Plinian eruption. It occurred about 2,000 years after the first one.

6940 BC: Mercato eruption
A caldera formed on the summit during this eruption. A smaller eruption had also occurred about 4,000 years before.

1800 BC: Avellino eruption
This destroyed several Bronze Age settlements, burying villages under a layer of pumice and ash.

217 BC
Ice core samples and reports of earthquakes and a "dimmed Sun" suggest an eruption possibly occurred during this year.

AD 79
The eruption altered the shape of the landscape and caused a mild tsunami in the Bay of Naples.

1. Afternoon

"The cloud was rising from a mountain ... [like] a pine tree. It rose into the sky on a very long 'trunk,' from which spread some 'branches.'"

2. Evening

"Ash was falling onto the ships now, darker and denser the closer they went. Now it was bits of pumice and rocks that were blackened and burned."

3. Following morning

"It wasn't long thereafter that the cloud stretched down to the ground and covered the sea. It girdled Capri and made it vanish."

Eyewitness account

The description by seventeen-year-old Pliny the Younger is the earliest eyewitness account of a volcanic eruption. He was on the opposite side of the Bay of Naples when Vesuvius exploded.

Ash turned to concrete
The giant plume of ash that spewed from Vesuvius was followed by water, which turned the ashfall into mud. Later, this turned to paste, then to natural concrete, which entombed everything within it.

DISASTER SITE
The eruption covered Pompeii in more than 10 feet (3 m) of ash. Herculaneum was closer to Vesuvius and it was buried under a thick layer of volcanic deposits up to 66 feet (20 m) deep. Many of the villages in the area were also destroyed.

Help to the region
In the months following the eruption, the Emperor Titus offered aid to the devastated region. Survivors returned to find a wasteland where their homes had been. Parts of buildings poked up through the ash and helped them work out where they had once lived.

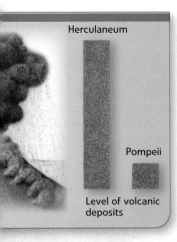

Herculaneum

Pompeii

Level of volcanic deposits

After the Eruption

Although thousands of people lost their lives when Vesuvius erupted, most of the residents of Pompeii managed to escape. Those who left in the first few hours after the eruption survived. Some people took only what they could carry. Others loaded up donkey carts and wagons with their belongings. Some people locked away their precious treasures, planning to retrieve them when they returned. They had no way of knowing that their homes would be buried under tons (t) of volcanic debris.

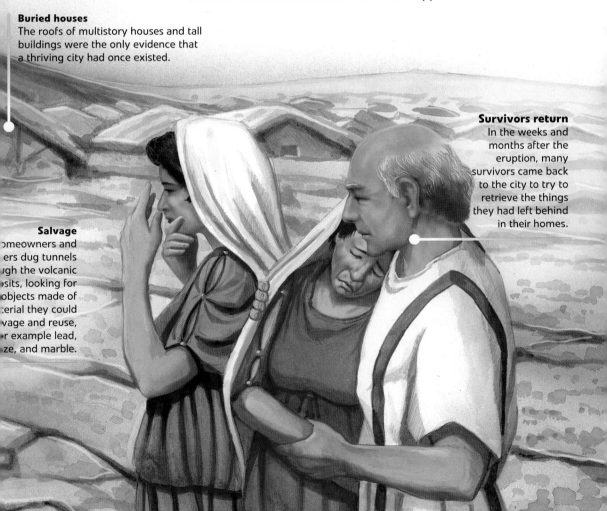

Buried houses
The roofs of multistory houses and tall buildings were the only evidence that a thriving city had once existed.

Survivors return
In the weeks and months after the eruption, many survivors came back to the city to try to retrieve the things they had left behind in their homes.

Salvage
Homeowners and others dug tunnels through the volcanic deposits, looking for objects made of material they could salvage and reuse, for example lead, bronze, and marble.

Making mosaic floors

Craftsmen used hammers and chisels to cut marble and sandstone into small tiles called tesserae. The tiles and pieces of glass were pressed into a bed of mortar to create a pattern or picture. Then the mosaic floor was cleaned and polished.

Amazing Discovery

Pompeii lay buried, abandoned, and forgotten for centuries. In 1599, men working in the Sarno River valley unearthed ancient walls covered with paintings. Not realizing their significance, an architect ordered them to be covered over again. In the following centuries, many more ruins were discovered, including those of the port town of Herculaneum in 1738. Although digging began at Pompeii in 1748, it was not until 1763 that an inscription on a statue identified the site as the famous lost city.

EXCAVATING MOSAICS

Archaeologists must excavate mosaics and paintings carefully to make sure these precious artworks are not damaged. Sometimes, a copy is made and installed in the original site. This was done for the Alexander Mosaic, discovered in the House of the Faun in Pompeii.

Many ... imagined ... that the universe was plunged into eternal darkness for evermore.

PLINY THE YOUNGER

Excavating the Victims

Although many citizens of Pompeii managed to escape, others were not so lucky. Some would have been too old or sick to travel. Others may have decided to ignore the warnings, or thought it was safer to stay in their homes until the eruption finished. These are the people whose "bodies" have now been retrieved from hardened ash tombs. The ash retained an imprint, or mold, of each body exactly as it was at the time of death. The clothes, flesh, and other soft parts decayed away.

Family group
Archaeological teams were able to carefully remove preserved bodies. Several family groups were discovered at Pompeii. A family of 13 was found crouched together in the back room of a large house. Another group was huddled on a staircase.

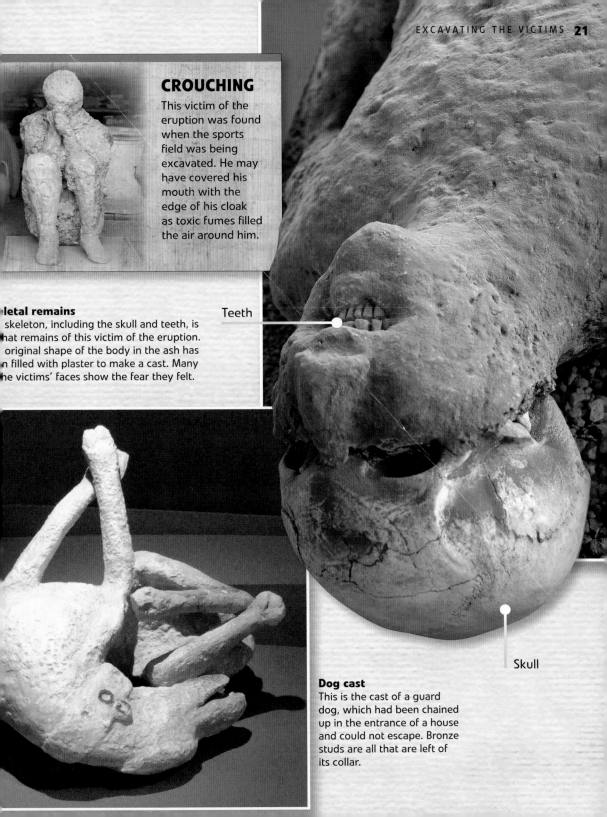

CROUCHING

This victim of the eruption was found when the sports field was being excavated. He may have covered his mouth with the edge of his cloak as toxic fumes filled the air around him.

Teeth

...letal remains

...skeleton, including the skull and teeth, is ...hat remains of this victim of the eruption. ...original shape of the body in the ash has ...n filled with plaster to make a cast. Many ...he victims' faces show the fear they felt.

Skull

Dog cast

This is the cast of a guard dog, which had been chained up in the entrance of a house and could not escape. Bronze studs are all that are left of its collar.

Creating a Cast

I n 1860, Italian archaeologist Giuseppe Fiorelli found a way to recreate the shapes of the bodies entombed in the hardened ash. He poured liquid plaster into the spaces left in the ash after the victims' flesh and clothing had decomposed. This technique was also used to make plaster casts of the doors, windows, and stairs of the houses. More recently, thanks to the work of archaeologists making casts of plant roots, some of Pompeii's gardens have been recreated, complete with flowers and fruit trees. Today, epoxy resin is often used instead of plaster.

A plaster cast works in the same way as a mold filled with gelatin.

Entombed body
Almost 2,000 people were suffocated and buried in the huge deposits of ash that fell on Pompeii. As the ash piled up, it set hard around their bodies, clothing, and jewelry, entombing them.

1

Frozen in position
Many bodies are still in the position they were in when the person died, with their hands shielding their face.

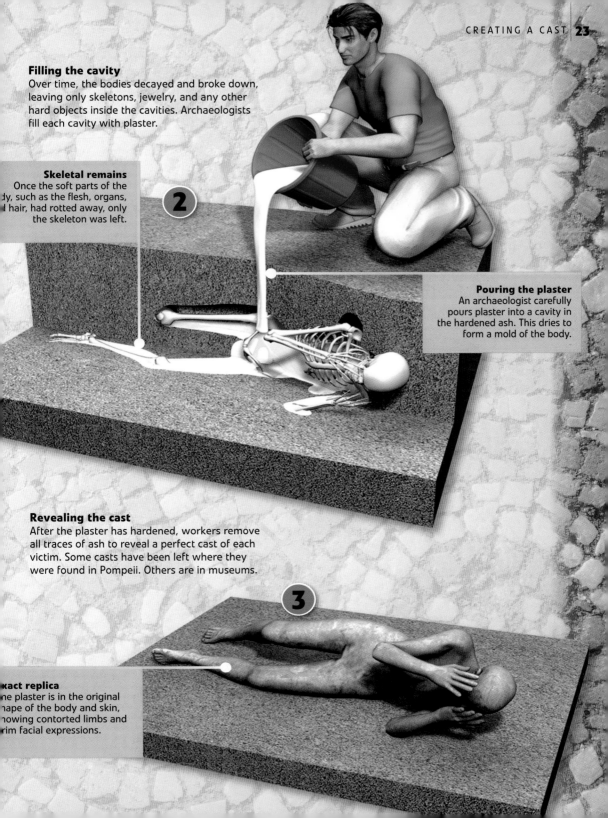

Filling the cavity
Over time, the bodies decayed and broke down, leaving only skeletons, jewelry, and any other hard objects inside the cavities. Archaeologists fill each cavity with plaster.

Skeletal remains
Once the soft parts of the ...dy, such as the flesh, organs, ... hair, had rotted away, only the skeleton was left.

2

Pouring the plaster
An archaeologist carefully pours plaster into a cavity in the hardened ash. This dries to form a mold of the body.

Revealing the cast
After the plaster has hardened, workers remove all traces of ash to reveal a perfect cast of each victim. Some casts have been left where they were found in Pompeii. Others are in museums.

3

...xact replica
...ne plaster is in the original
...ape of the body and skin,
...owing contorted limbs and
...rim facial expressions.

Reconstructing the Past

Archaeologists have now uncovered about two thirds of the city. The buildings and the objects they contain help us to imagine what life would have been like in the years before Mount Vesuvius erupted. Frescoes painted on the walls show scenes from daily life, including what the people looked like and how they dressed. The houses of wealthy people had an area called a peristyle. This informal living area consisted of a covered area with columns that was surrounded by a garden or courtyard.

Cubiculum
This small room was used as a bedroom.

Atrium
The sunlight from a hole in the roof lit this space.

Storage room

Houses of Pompeii

The houses were different from today's houses. The living rooms faced inward and had no windows. In the middle of the house, a large atrium (central room) with highly decorated walls was lit by natural light from a hole in the roof.

Inside a house
This reconstruction of the House of Venus shows an interior wall of the peristyle, which is decorated in vivid frescoes and bordered with stone columns.

Facial reconstruction
Using a computer program, bones from a skull, and Roman artwork, archaeologists have reconstructed the faces of those found at Pompeii.

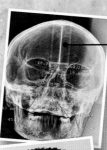

Skull
The skull is the starting point for reconstruction.

Details
Hairstyle and eye color are taken from paintings.

dra
was a large
munal room.

CEIVM SECUNDVM

Outdoor garden

Peristyle
This was an informal living area.

SKULL SECRETS

A scientist examines an excavated skull. She is looking for clues about people's size, diet, and health 2,000 years ago.

Excavated skull

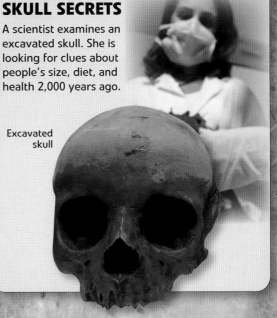

Frescoes

A fresco was made by applying a layer of wet plaster onto a wall or panel. Rich color was added to an outline while the plaster was still wet. The Pompeii frescoes are a snapshot of life back then.

Treasure from Tragedy

Not only bodies have been recovered from the excavation of Pompeii. The volcanic ash also preserved items such as bronze and marble sculptures, gold jewelry, armor, coins, mosaics, and frescoes. They reveal a great deal about the people of Pompeii, their belongings, and their life in the Bay of Naples during the early days of the Roman Empire.

Marble emperor

This bust shows the head of the young Tiberius (42 BC–AD 37). He was the second emperor of Rome, ruling from AD 14 to 37. Many wealthy people displayed marble busts of important people in the atrium of their house.

Head protection

The grille of linked circles on this bronze helmet protected the gladiator's face. The brim protected the back and sides of his head. The medallion of Hercules was a symbol of strength and victory.

Coiled snake

The coiled snake on this pure gold armlet was a symbol of immortality. Ancient Romans also thought snakes brought good luck. Images of snakes guarded springs and homes and were used for decorating bracelets.

Gladiator's dagger

This bronze dagger was found at the gladiators' barracks. Most gladiators were slaves or prisoners of war. They were trained to fight each other to the death for the entertainment of the public.

Silver treasure

Valuable items such as this silver drinking cup have been found strewn around houses or hidden in stairwells. Residents bundled up whatever they could carry in their rush to escape.

Gods and goddesses

Recovered from a house in Herculaneum, this wall mosaic depicts the Roman god Neptune and the goddess Venus. Many of the best mosaics copied old Greek paintings, which were painted on wood panels.

Visiting Pompeii Today

The excavation of Pompeii has allowed us to see what everyday life was like in a Roman city 2,000 years ago. Walking along the excavated streets and through the ruins of the buildings, it is possible to imagine busy shoppers in the marketplace, or people reclining on couches or relaxing in heated baths, gossiping or talking politics with friends and family. You can almost hear the clash of metal as the gladiators battled it out in the arena, or smell the bread baking in the bakery ovens.

Restaurant
Cracked steps, a crumbling wall, and stone slabs are all that is left of a restaurant. Patrons came here to relax, play games, and feast on delicacies.

Theater
The open-air theater was similar to an ancient Greek theater. It had a series of steps on which the audience sat, and an area for the actors and the scenery.

Bronze statue

Mount Vesuvius

Paved streets
Streets and sidewalks were mainly paved in basalt, a volcanic rock that is hard, smooth, and very slippery when wet. Stepping stones in the streets helped pedestrians to cross.

Thermal baths
The public baths had one section for men and one for women. Bathers usually moved through a series of heated rooms that became progressively hotter. There were also changing rooms and toilets.

Bakery
Archaeologists have found 33 bakeries in Pompeii. One still had a few loaves of bread, now carbonized. This means the oven must have been in use when the volcano erupted.

Time capsule
Pompeii is a time capsule of ancient Roman life. You can walk the streets, visit the arena, theater, and houses, view the statues, frescoes, and mosaics, and even climb Mount Vesuvius.

Make Your Own Volcano

Make your own version of Mount Vesuvius and watch it erupt.

1. Spread out the clothes or newspaper on a floor, table, or other flat surface. Place the plastic bottle on the pie pan or baking pan.

2. Construct a volcano shape around the bottle with the modeling clay. Ensure the clay does not cover or go into the top of the bottle.

3. Using the funnel, spoon the baking soda into the bottle.

4. Add a few drops of dishwashing liquid, followed by the water, to the bottle.

5. Put the vinegar into a small bowl, then add a few drops of the food coloring to the vinegar.

6. Using the funnel, carefully pour the colored vinegar mixture into the bottle. Remove the funnel immediately.

7. Stand back as your volcano erupts!

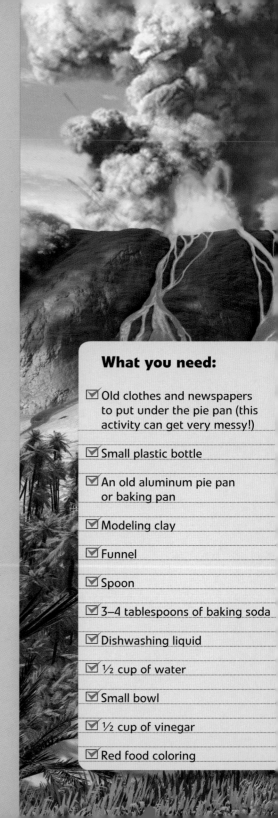

What you need:

- ☑ Old clothes and newspapers to put under the pie pan (this activity can get very messy!)
- ☑ Small plastic bottle
- ☑ An old aluminum pie pan or baking pan
- ☑ Modeling clay
- ☑ Funnel
- ☑ Spoon
- ☑ 3–4 tablespoons of baking soda
- ☑ Dishwashing liquid
- ☑ ½ cup of water
- ☑ Small bowl
- ☑ ½ cup of vinegar
- ☑ Red food coloring

lossary

ueducts (A-kweh-dukts)

ficial channels that carry
er from one place to another.

onze Age (BRONZ AYJ)

eriod of time between the
e Age and the Iron Age,
n weapons and tools
e made of bronze.

dera (kal-DER-uh)

rge crater formed by
lcanic explosion or the
pse of a volcanic cone.

valry (KA-vul-ree)

liers trained to fight
norseback.

ris (duh-BREE)

ble or wreckage.

oxy resin
PAHK-see REH-zin)

gh, adhesive material used
nake protective coatings
glues.

cavate (EK-skuh-vayt)

emove by digging
cooping out.

fresco (FRES-koh)

A wall painting where watercolor
has been applied to wet plaster.

gladiators
(GLA-dee-ay-turz)

Men who entertained the public
by fighting, usually to the death,
other men or animals in an arena.

immortality
(ih-mor-TAH-lih-tee)

Endless life.

lava (LAH-vuh)

Molten rock that flows from a
volcano or crack in Earth's crust.

mosaic (moh-ZAY-ik)

A surface decoration made by
setting small pieces of colored
stone, glass, or tile in mortar.

plebeians (plih-BEE-unz)

Average or common Roman
citizens, usually thought
of as lower class.

pumice (PUH-mus)

Very light volcanic rock,
full of cavities.

pyroclastic flow
(py-roh-KLAS-tik FLOH)

A ground-hugging avalanche of
hot ash, pumice, rock fragments,
and volcanic gas that rushes
down the side of a volcano.

Roman Empire
(ROH-mun EM-py-ur)

Roman territories that, at the
empire's peak, stretched from
Britain and Germany to the
Persian Gulf and North Africa.

salvage (SAL-vij)

To save damaged or discarded
material for further use.

tectonic plates
(tek-TAH-nik PLAYTZ)

Large plates of rock that make
up the foundation of Earth's
crust, and which are the source
of earthquakes.

tesserae (TEH-suh-ree)

Small cubes of stone, glass,
or tile used to make mosaics.

toga (TOH-guh)

A loose, one-piece outer garment
worn in public by male citizens
in ancient Rome.

Index

Websites

Due to the changing nature of Internet links, PowerKids Press has developed an online list of websites related to the subject of this book. This site is updated regularly. Please use this link to access the list: www.powerkidslinks.com/disc/pomp/